PETER KAY
BIOGRAPHY BOOK

The Untold Story of His Comedy Career Success

By Ann Hughes

Table of Contents

Foreword

In the world of comedy, there are those who make us laugh, and then there's Peter Kay. With a wit as sharp as his northern accent and a humor that transcends borders, Peter Kay has earned his place as a beloved and iconic figure in the realm of stand-up comedy. In this book, we embark on a journey through the life and career of a man who has brought joy to millions. From his humble beginnings in Bolton to filling arenas with laughter, Peter's story is one of talent, resilience, and an unwavering dedication to making people smile.

As we delve into the pages ahead, you'll gain insights into the man behind the laughter, exploring the influences and experiences that have shaped his unique comedic style. You'll discover the characters, catchphrases, and moments that have become etched into our collective memory, reminding us that laughter is indeed the best medicine.

Whether you're a die-hard Peter Kay fan or simply someone who appreciates the power of humor to brighten our lives, this book offers a deeper understanding of the comedian who has left an indelible mark on the world of entertainment. So, sit back, relax, and prepare to relive the laughs, the tears, and the unforgettable moments that define the extraordinary career of Peter Kay.

In the world of comedy, there's a name that resonates with audiences of all ages, a name synonymous with uproarious laughter and heartwarming humor—Peter Kay.

Introduction

Welcome to a journey through the life and career of a comedy icon, a man who has charmed his way into our hearts, one punchline at a time. In these pages, we'll uncover the man behind the mic, exploring the origins of his humor, the triumphs that have defined his career, and the genuine warmth that has endeared him to millions.

From his early days in the heart of Bolton to commanding the grandest stages, Peter Kay's story is one of passion, persistence, and the unmistakable ability to find hilarity in the everyday. We'll relive the bellyaches of laughter brought on by his memorable stand-up performances, from garlic bread to car-sharing, and everything in between.

But this isn't just a book about comedy; it's a celebration of the power of laughter to unite us, to heal us, and to remind us that, no matter what life throws our way, there's always room for a good laugh. So, join us as we dive into the world of Peter Kay—a world where laughter knows no boundaries and where humor is the universal language.

Prepare to laugh, reminisce, and rediscover the joy that Peter Kay has brought into our lives. It's time to celebrate the laughter legacy of a true comedy legend.

Chapter 1

The Early years - Peter Kay Humble Beginning

July 2, 1973 marked Peter Kay's birth. During the year 2018, he turns 45. Peter was born in Farnworth, Lancashire, even though he frequently refers to Bolton as his hometown. Irish-born Roman Catholic Deirdre is the mother of Peter Kay, who was raised in that religion. Just as his professional career was about to take off, his father Michael, an engineer, passed away. Susan Gargan is the spouse of Peter Kay. Since Peter's family wants to keep their private lives private, nothing is known about her life outside of the spotlight. In 1998, she happened to meet her spouse in a club in Bolton.

Peter was reportedly working at the neighborhood movie theater and Susan was reportedly working at their neighborhood Boots. After three years of dating, they got hitched in 2001.

Charlie Michael Kay, a teenager, is the son of Peter and Susan. He was given the names Charlie and John after their deceased fathers, John being Susan's father. Thought to have two further children, they have been incredibly secretive about their upbringing. In 2018, Peter Kay was scheduled to embark on his first tour in eight years, however due to personal reasons, he had to postpone 100 dates. From April 2018 to June 2019, he had intended to travel and play in nine locations across the UK. He remarked, "I profoundly regret that I am having to cancel all of my upcoming business assignments due to unanticipated family difficulties.

Peter Kay has had a lot of chart success, in fact! Three of his songs have reached the top spot: his cover of The Proclaimers' "500 Miles" as Brian Potter with the "Little Britain" stars in 2005, his re-release of Tony Christie's "Is This the Way to Amarillo?" in 2006, and his "Children in Need Medley" (as Peter Kay's All-Star Animated Band). He also had three top 20 singles as Geraldine McQueen, one of which was a Susan Boyle-featuring duet.

Peter Kay's Childhood

Fans of Peter Kay are overjoyed that he is returning. The comedian's new "Better Late Than Never" tour tickets are now available, and ticket websites are already having trouble keeping up with demand. With Peter making his first theatrical appearance in 12 years, it's one of the most anxiously awaited performances in British comedy history. Even though Peter is well-liked across the nation, anyone who is familiar with his work understands that he is fiercely proud of his Boltonian heritage. Many of his stand-up routines make reference to his beloved hometown of Bolton, and shows like That Peter Kay Thing and Phoenix Nights are all set there. We've looked back at how one of Bolton's favorite sons got his start as excitement for the comedian's upcoming tour grows.

Peter was raised in the Croston Street neighborhood of the Daubhill neighborhood, a very congested street with terraced homes on either side. It shares a lot of characteristics with other streets in the vicinity. In the previous 20 years, homes in the neighborhood have averaged just £60,000 in cost while selling for as little as £12,000. It might be hard to imagine that one of the more costly homes on the street was only purchased two years ago for a mere £78,000, yet the residence once belonged to one of the nation's most popular comedians. There aren't many of Peter Kay's former neighbors left on the street, and one of the few people who still reside there told the Manchester Evening News that he was utterly unaware of his neighbor's humorous abilities until he saw him on television. "I didn't really know who he was until he did Phoenix Nights," he claimed. We moved in a few years before he went, and I didn't get to know him all that well; all we really did was see him by the house on his way to church and other such things. I'm not sure if any of his former neighbors are still on this block.

He was once known by one of my friends, however he recently passed away. He departed after getting married but would occasionally return to visit his mother. Peter Kay describes his time in school at Mount St. Joseph Secondary School and St. Ethelbert's Primary School, both of which were about a five-minute walk from his Croston Street home, in his excellent autobiography "The Sound of Laughter." Peter made fun of the fact that both schools were administered by nuns by saying "nuns and showbiz don't mix." He did, however, get his first taste of entertaining an audience when in Class 3 at St. Ethelbert's when he portrayed an innkeeper in the yearly nativity play. Peter recalls that the audience 'liked it' when he deviated from the script and offered Mary and Joseph 'an en-suite with full English'. What a lovely sensation it is to be on stage and hear laughing, the author said in his essay. I felt content and secure. After graduating from St. Ethelbert's, he enrolled in Mount St. Joseph, a secondary school with a convent setting that was established in 1902 by the Sisters of the Cross and Passion.

Peter disguises the nuns' identity in The Sound of Laughter by giving them amusing nicknames like "Sister Sledge" and "Sister Act 2." The nuns who taught Peter while he was a student at the school were interviewed by The Manchester Evening News. Peter's ninth-grade chemistry teacher, a nun, said that he was "never any trouble." Another claimed that because of the comedian's masterful "ad libbing," she frequently "crossed swords" with him. She claimed that if he did it in theater class, it frequently confused the other students. The Sound of Laughter makes mention of one such instance of his 'ad libbing'. Peter states that while portraying the Cowardly Lion in The Wizard of Oz, he deviated from the script by cocking up his leg and acting as though he had to urinate on stage. During his time in school, Peter worked his first of many jobs, delivering the Bolton Evening News for £3.50 a week.

Due to the effort of carrying the newspapers on his back, he made light of the fact that his body is now a "walking time bomb." Peter eventually departed Mount St. Joseph, and the school moved to Greenland Road in Farnworth. Al Jamiatul Islamiyah, a boarding school, now resides in the original convent structure. Peter held a number of jobs between graduating from Mount St. Joseph and making his comic debut, the majority of which served as the basis for his material. He has held several jobs throughout the years, including those at a toilet paper factory, an Esso garage, a bingo hall, a movie theater, the Manchester Arena, and more. But it's safe to assume Bolton will always hold a special place in his heart, no matter where his career leads him next.

Chapter 2

The Rise to Fame: How Peter Kay Became a Household Name

Michael John Kay, HiKay's father, was an engineer, but he passed away before Kay's career as an entertainer really took off and he was propelled to fame. Kay was raised in the faith of his mother, Margaret, an Irish Catholic who was originally from Coalisland in County Tyrone. Before he became well-known, Kay worked a variety of part-time jobs, including those at a toilet paper factory, a Netto supermarket, Manchester Arena, a cash and carry, a movie theater, a gas station, and a bingo hall. These positions later served as the inspiration for episodes of That Peter Kay Thing.

He began a degree program in theater, theatre studies, and English literature at the University of Liverpool. After struggling with the curriculum, he went to the Higher National Diploma (HND) in media performance, including stand-up, at the University of Salford's Adelphi Campus School of Media, Music, and Performance. Kay earned an honorary Doctor of Arts degree from Salford University on July 19, 2016, at Salford's Lowry Theatre in recognition of his work in the entertainment industry. He achieved his first triumph in stand-up comedy in the North West Comedian of the Year competition, which was held in Manchester and was hosted by Dave Spikey, subsequently the co-star and co-writer of Phoenix Nights. Despite being last on the schedule, Kay won the match against Johnny Vegas. While working part-time as an usher at his local Bolton movie theater, he continued to perform stand-up locally. After the theater closed, he had the choice of finding another job or dedicating himself to comedy.

After competing in and winning Channel 4's So You Think You're Funny? competition in 1997, he gave his first semi-pro stand-up performances at the 1998 Edinburgh Fringe Festival, earning him a prestigious Perrier Award nomination. Kay said in November 2009 that he will return to stand-up comedy in April of the following year with a performance titled The Tour That Doesn't Tour Tour...Now On Tour after a seven-year absence. Due to the overwhelming demand for tickets, he swiftly announced that the performance will go on tour. The tour, which drew 1.2 million viewers, was acknowledged by the Guinness Book of World Records as the greatest stand-up comedy tour of all time in January 2012.While Kay's tour received some light press criticism, his disabled supporters had to pay up to £39 on premium phone lines to buy tour tickets.

By announcing his first tour in eight years in November 2017, Kay indicated intentions to resume doing stand-up comedy. The Peter Kay Live: Have Gags, Will Travel tour was scheduled to launch in April 2018 at the Genting Arena and stop at venues like the SSE Hydro. Plans for the tour's beginning in

2018 were announced. On December 13, 2017, Kay decided to put a stop to all forthcoming professional pursuits, including the Peter Kay Live: Have Gags Will Travel tour, citing family obligations. He had asked for the media to respect his and his family's privacy. In 2016, Kay won the BAFTA TV Award for Best Scripted Comedy.

First Foray into Stand Up Comedy

With his first live tour in 12 years, Peter Kay has announced his comeback to live stand-up comedy. The 49-year-old comedian, who has spent the past four years largely hidden from the public eye, will start an arena tour in December that will stretch until August of 2023. It will be his first live tour since 2010, when he performed for more than 1.2 million spectators and set the Guinness World Record for the greatest selling run of all time. His return was revealed during an I'm A Celebrity! series premiere commercial break. Later on, he'll be in Birmingham, Liverpool, Sheffield, Belfast, Newcastle, Glasgow, and Dublin. At the Sheffield Utilita Arena, on August 11, 2023, his reign will come to an end. After the news, Kay's official website briefly seemed to crash due to a spike in online traffic. A ticket to one of Kay's performances was referred to as the "ideal Christmas gift" on a poster for the occasion, which portrayed Kay holding a sign that read, "Better late than never. "Kay, a native of Bolton, has mostly faded from public view in recent years.

In August 2021, he made a special comeback to the stage for two charity performances to support Laura Nuttall, a 20-year-old who was suffering from the severe brain cancer glioblastoma multiforme. A brief return occurred in January 2021 when he spoke with Cat Deeley, who was taking over for Graham Norton on BBC Radio 2, on his love of music, mixtapes, and the musical Mamma Mia. In 2018, he also unexpectedly showed up at a charity screening of his television series Car Share. In December 2017, Kay canceled his most recent tour, citing "unforeseen family circumstances". With his popular, Bafta-winning television series Car Share and stand-up performances over the past few years, Kay has pleased viewers.

While eager fans waited in line around the block to see the Bolton comedian's return to the stage, Peter Kay was pictured arriving for his comeback performances in Manchester. When the Car Share and Phoenix Nights star announced two very special gigs in his hometown—his first onstage appearance in three years—he set up a frenzy. The well-liked comedian recently stepped away from the spotlight, but he recently returned for two Q&A performances at the Manchester O2 Apollo. The 48-year-old is raising money for Laura Nuttall, 21, of Pendle, Lancashire, who is facing grade four brain cancer and glioblastoma. When Laura first started having headaches at the age of 18, she assumed she had the 'freshers' flu' but was subsequently found to have six inoperable brain tumors.

Two and a half years after receiving her diagnosis, the inspirational young woman, an advocate for the Brain Tumour Charity, has finished her second year of study at Manchester University. She underwent two brain operations, 30 radiotherapy treatments, and 12 months of chemotherapy. Peter will give Laura, who is in the audience with her family, all of the proceeds from his two "Doing It For Laura" performances—a matinee and an evening show. When tickets went on sale, both events were completely sold out in under 30 minutes.

Along with her mother Nicola, Laura came on This Morning on Tuesday to speak with broadcasters Eamonn Holmes and Ruth Langsford. She talked about how a family friend who is one of the most popular comedians in the UK made a comeback to save her life. Nicola went on to describe how Peter called Mark, her husband. It was actually a major surprise, she remarked.

Laura was initially diagnosed with a brain tumor in 2018, and has since received treatment in Germany. But in March, the cancer came back. Immunotherapy is what I'm receiving in Germany, according to Laure, and this treatment is unavailable in the UK. The procedure is "phenomenally expensive," Nicola continued, and the family has been "slogging away" at fundraising ever since learning about it.

Chapter 3

Peter's Subsequent Success: The Breakthrough Moment

BOLTON cartoon It was jokingly referred to as the "My Mum Wants A Bungalow" was a comedy tour by Peter Kay. But there has been such a high demand for tickets that Deirdre Kay, who was once modest, could now afford to purchase a complete neighborhood of one-story houses. Since comedy's "man of the moment" began touring in September of last year, an astounding 380,000 tickets have been occupied. And with top-tier tickets going for $25, the 180-date marathon has made somewhere around $5 million. It came to a close on July 1 with the first-ever stand-up performance at the Manchester Evening News Arena, which is also the venue where, ironically, Kay once looked on with admiration as a steward wearing a yellow jacket.

By the time I had finished my stay there, I was performing stand-up. I completed in 1999, however it was a fantastic work. Simply work the evenings you wanted to see that show, which I did. I performed all 10 of them, and my favorite was Take That. The demand for "My Mum" tour tickets indicates that Kay has surpassed the former Manchester boy band in popularity. However, unlike Take That, who were toned, gorgeous, and untouchable, Kay's tubby brand of broad-accented humour is focused solely on the everyday, such as ice cream salesmen.

One of the six documentaries was the pilot for Phoenix Nights, the Farnworth-set comedy that gave Kay's most well-known character, the boss who uses a wheelchair, Brian Potter, and has since had two successful seasons. In the 2002 Madchester film 24 Hour Party People, he played Don Tonay, the sleazy owner of The Factory Club in Hulme, the forerunner of the Hacienda, and filled in for Johnny Vaughan on The Big Breakfast. He also had a walk-on role in Coronation Street. Although London or perhaps Hollywood may be appealing, Kay is now deeply devoted to his Bolton origins. Prior to marrying Susan Gargan, a redhead Boots cashier he met in a Bolton nightclub before he became well-known, he continued to live at home in Daubhill with his mother.

He claims that the town serves as inspiration for most of his humour and that he would rather give up his job than move. He says, "Bolton is home, and everything is normal." "I like that no one ever treats me differently. I don't dislike London; I just question why we have to travel there. I enjoy staying at home. Family and friends come first in life. Deirdre has been scrutinizing Peter's jokes for his whole career, so if she is currently touring Bolton real estate offices with a sizable check in her hand, then she undoubtedly deserves it. His father, Michael, passed away three years ago at the age of 51, and his parents split amicably while he was a teenager.

Sadly, Dad did not live to see the success of Phoenix Nights, the TV show that Peter co-wrote and that helped his career advance. He recalls that due to osteoporosis, his father had retired early from his position as an engineer. But nothing can get you ready for this. Because Dad was such a big part of my act and I used to mention him all the time, I stopped doing any more shows. As the roly-poly face of John Smith's bitter, Kay has gained even more admirers.

The Commonwealth Games were held in Manchester last year, and a memorable television commercial that ran throughout the event had Kay belly-flopping into an Olympic-sized swimming pool. When he came out of the water, his trunks were drooping, and the commentator called him "top bombing" as the judges held out cards with high ratings. Items that may be purchased from Kay's well-known merchandising website also feature other well-known catchphrases. The website sells items including T-shirts with the catchphrases "Get on the Internet" and "Put Big Light On," automobile decals for Chorley FM, and an apron with the phrase "Garlic Bread."

On the Tower's Roof

His Top Of The Tower video undoubtedly ended up on thousands of wish lists for Christmas presents. Despite the fact that he just turned 30 and may be seen by some as a late bloomer, Kay was always destined to be a performer. Apparently, he would rather entertain those around him than complete his job, according to a school report from when he was five or six years old .At Mount St. Joseph's Catholic School in Bolton, he caused havoc as the Cowardly Lion when he was 15 years old. He remembers, "I continued and cocked me leg up on a tree." "The nuns in charge of the school lost it. But the audience as a whole laughed, and I was overjoyed. When I began doing stand-up, that feeling returned the following time. Peter graduated from Mount St. Joseph's with a single art GCSE. He continued on to Bolton College to complete a BTEC in Performing Arts while working a variety of part-time jobs, including packing toilet paper, serving drinks, being an usher at the ABC Cinema in Bolton, and being a mobile DJ.

He then made the decision that he wanted to pursue a degree and lied about his credentials to enroll in a course in American history at Liverpool University. "I dislike discussing it. I applied for a degree program, stating that I had two A-levels and five GCSEs, and was accepted. Never once did anyone care to inquire about my credentials. After having trouble with the work, he went to Salford University's HND program in Media Performance and Performing Arts, which helped establish his comic career. I decided to pursue stand-up comedy, he says. You were required to do a spot at the neighborhood bar, The Pint Pot, where the tutors would arrive and grade you based on the audience's response. Favorably, it was favorably received. I made the decision to use the remaining 10 minutes before I departed to create a set that I could submit for the City Life North West Comedian of the Year Award. A few months later, at the age of 23, and with only four prior public appearances, Kay won the contest.

"When I won, I couldn't believe it. After that, I recall being at my grandmother's house and hearing someone on the phone say, "I can give you £30," to which I thought, "Bloody hell, £30 for 20 minutes." For £42.50 an hour, I used to work a whole week at the theater. There wasn't much you could teach Peter, concedes Lloyd Peters, senior lecturer in media and performance at Salford University, who oversaw the comedy course. In reality, he was constantly assisting others with their performance.

"I believe his working-class background is what has given him the maturity I have never before seen in a pupil. "He views things as comic material that most students might disregard, like the kind of pop they sell at Netto, where he worked. He also possesses a remarkable memory for television theme songs and stories, which he could only have acquired by watching television for countless hours. He has devoted hours to researching personalities like Les Dawson, who he frequently draws comparisons to.

The stage

He is viewed as friendly and cuddly thanks to his features, which also helps. I believe that the Peter Kay on stage is the real one. He is aware of the entire working class culture. He usually makes fun of people with tenderness, but in my opinion, that is when he is most effective. In fact, Kay's ability to make others laugh through observation has gotten him into trouble. Keith Laird, a fire safety officer for Bolton, is said to have received £10,000 in damages when Phoenix Nights included a Keith Lard figure doing a similar job.

The similarities, including Lard's tagline "Ignorance kills, not fire," were, in Kay's opinion, purely coincidental. Additionally, he made a crude joke about Jill Dando, which drew angry media attention to him. Although he enjoys taking risks, he asserts that he wouldn't be too worried if he ever found himself back among regular Bolton residents. He argues, "Money is nothing to me. "I've never had much money. In the end, I'd prefer to continue doing what I'm doing, but if things don't work out, I'll just sign on or go back to the bins. And if the trash cans won't take him, he can always rely on the money from his mother's home.

Chapter 4

The Stand Up Specials

The O2 stadium in London will host Peter Kay's new stand-up show on a monthly basis for a whole calendar year. Here are five of his funniest performances.

With the sale of more than 1.2 million tickets, Kay's UK tour in 2010–11 set the Guinness World Record for the most successful standup tour. Nearly 10 million people have watched his misheard lyrics routine on YouTube. I was singing "wash your back" instead of "want you back" in Take That's "Back for Good," claims Kay. In Sister Sledge's song "We Are Family," the phrase "state for the record" was misheard as "staple the vicar".

Kay also used it in his stand-up performances. I can already taste it; it's the future. When speaking on a talk show in 2017, Kay claimed that people were still yelling "garlic bread" at him on the street because the joke had gained such notoriety. Kay famously illustrated what each family member was like during a wedding during one of his stand-up performances. Kay slipped across the floor on his knees, doing what "little lads" do at weddings.

In a sketch, Kay made fun of how when it starts to rain, the schoolyard turns into a bloodbath, and how grownups would say, "It's the fine rain that soaks you through," while equating their attempts to send kids inside with Saving Private Ryan. He claimed that they could smell the rain and sense it.

In a 2005 video, Kay can be seen miming to Tony Christie's 1971 hit song Is This the Way to Amarillo while sporting a beautiful purple outfit. After the video's popularity, the song was re-released to support Comic Relief, featuring Peter Kay on the track, and it became a UK No 1. In 2020, Kay reenacted the famous video with members of the British public as part of a Comic Relief fundraising event.

Peter Kay has achieved extraordinary comedic success in the television industry. He is well recognized for producing and co-starring in a number of acclaimed TV programs. Following are a few of Peter Kay's standout TV appearances and comedic accomplishments:

Peter Kay co-wrote and performed in the cult comedy series Phoenix Nights (2001–2002), which was set in a working men's club. His role of club owner Brian Potter rose to fame, and the program won praise from critics. Max and Paddy's Road to Nowhere (2004): This "Phoenix Nights" spin-off followed the exploits of the Max and Paddy characters as they toured the country in their campervan. For Kay and his co-star Paddy McGuinness, it was yet another success.

That Peter Kay Thing (2000): A collection of stand-alone comic dramas, this was Kay's first step into television. It displayed his comic prowess and adaptability.

(2015–2018) Peter Kay's Car Share Peter Kay contributed to the writing and co-creation of this wildly successful sitcom. It centered on the amusing interactions between two coworkers as they traveled to and from work each day. The compilation show Peter Kay's Comedy Shuffle (2016–2018) offers a look back at some of Kay's funniest sketches and stand-up routines throughout his career.

Peter Kay is well-known for his stand-up comedy in addition to his work in television. His live performances, such as "Live at the Top of the Tower" and "The Tour That Didn't Tour Tour," have set records and won praise from critics. Peter Kay has achieved enormous success in television and comedy thanks to his distinctive humorous style, approachable humor, and capacity to capture the essence of everyday life. He has grown to be a beloved character in British comedy, and audiences all around the world continue to chuckle at his work.

Chapter 5

Beyond Comedy and the Struggles

Peter Kay was raised in Bolton, England, where he was born. His humorous style, which frequently revolves around relatable, daily situations, is greatly influenced by his working-class upbringing and Northern English heritage.   Kay started his career as a stand-up comedian, honing his craft in comedy clubs. He rapidly became well-known for his observational wit and capacity to discover funny in the everyday.

Beyond comedy, Kay is also a gifted writer in addition to being a performer. Many of his television programs, such as "Phoenix Nights" and "Max and Paddy's Road to Nowhere," were co-written by him. The success of these projects was significantly influenced by his creative input.

His comedic performances have had a big cultural impact on the UK. His place in British comic history is cemented by the fact that words and phrases from his programs have entered common usage.

Kay is well-known for his comedic character in public, but he prefers to keep things quiet in private, giving his personal life a sense of mystery. Peter Kay has an enduring legacy thanks to his contributions to humor. His contributions are still lauded, and the British entertainment industry continues to adore him.

Peter Kay is a comedian who has made a significant contribution to the field of comedy by using his ability to connect with audiences profoundly. He has a keen understanding of the humor found in everyday life.

Like many comics, Peter Kay struggled to find success in the comedy world. He played in intimate settings in front of occasionally hostile crowds.

Given his private nature, balancing his stand-up profession with his family life and other commitments has probably offered its own unique set of obstacles. Following the success of "Phoenix Nights," there might have been pressure to produce similarly successful follow-up projects. Peter Kay stated in 2017 that his "Dance for Life" charity tour had to be canceled due to "unforeseen family circumstances."

Without a question, Peter Kay's greatest achievement is his enormous success in the comedic field. Because of his approachable humor and enduring personalities, he has emerged as one of the UK's most cherished and significant comedians. His stand-up tours, such as "The Tour That Didn't Tour Tour" and "Mum Wants a Bungalow Tour," shattered sales records, illustrating his popularity and attraction.

Peter Kay's series, such "Phoenix Nights" and "Peter Kay's Car Share," gained positive reviews and a devoted following. His contributions to television have had a long-lasting impact on British humor. Peter Kay's involvement in charitable causes,

44

especially those that benefit cancer patients, demonstrates his altruistic side and his willingness to use his popularity for good.

Kay has won various honors, including British humour Awards and National Television Awards, for his contributions to humour. Despite obstacles, Peter Kay's brilliance, genuineness, and audience-connection skills have produced a string of successes that have cemented his status as a comic legend in the UK.

Chapter 6

Peter Kay Comedy Style

Peter Kay is renowned for his accessible and insightful humor. He frequently finds humor in banal circumstances and everyday life, making his audience laugh at something they can instantly identify with. His comedic style is distinguished by clever storytelling, amusing accents, and a kind, approachable demeanor. His ability to find humor in the banal has won him fans among audiences in the UK and elsewhere.

Peter Kay is a master at noting the peculiarities and eccentricities of daily life and turning them into amusing anecdotes. He lends a humorous perspective to relatable everyday circumstances, such as going to the grocery store or coping with family gatherings.

Peter Kay's humour is known for its relatability. He frequently draws on shared feelings and experiences, which makes a wide range of people able to enjoy his humor. His relatability fosters a feeling of intimacy between him and his audience.

Peter Kay's humor primarily centers on observing daily life and the peculiarities of human behavior, which is known as observational comedy. He has a strong eye for the everyday details of life that are often overlooked yet begging to be explored comedically. He uses familiar events and gives them a hilarious spin to make audiences laugh.

A large portion of Peter Kay's humor is nostalgic, particularly in reference to his own working-class childhood in England. He frequently reflects on the past, remembering events from his youth, family get-togethers, and pop culture from the 1980s and 1990s. His audience responds to this nostalgia since many of them can identify with these common memories.

Character-Based Humor, In his stand-up acts, Kay is renowned for developing amusing characters and personas. His peculiar accents, mannerisms, and anecdotes give these characters life. These personas frequently represent exaggerated representations of regular people, which gives his performances an additional dimension of humor.

Kay's humor frequently incorporates storytelling. He has a talent for using common occurrences or personal tales to weave fascinating stories. The audience is drawn into his world and given the impression that they are experiencing his experiences thanks to his narrative skills, which make his routines seem more like conversations.

Peter Kay's humor tends to be clean and family-friendly, unlike some comedians who rely on shock value or obscene material. His comedy is understandable to a wide audience, including kids and elderly individuals, because he stays away from profanity and contentious topics.

Chapter 7

The Achievements: Peter Kay's Award and Recognition

Awards for Best Stand-Up Comedian and Best Comedy Entertainment Personality are among the many British Comedy Awards that Peter Kay has received over the years. He has won a number of awards, including the most popular comedy performer and the most popular entertainment program for "Peter Kay's Car Share. For his work in comedy and television shows, Peter Kay has been nominated for and won BAFTA Television Awards.

He has been honored by the Royal Television Society, which has given him prizes for Best Entertainment Performance. In 1997, at the Edinburgh Festival Fringe, Peter Kay took home the renowned Perrier Comedy Award, which helped launch his career. In appreciation of his great contributions to the arts and entertainment, he was awarded an honorary Doctor of Arts degree by the University of Salford.

His Numerous Influence on comedy

Peter Kay is renowned for his observational comedy, in which he amusingly remarks on daily life and universal experiences. Many comedians who likewise concentrate on the humor present in the everyday aspects of life might be attributed to this kind of comedy. A large audience can enjoy Kay's comedy because it frequently features issues and circumstances that can be related to. He established a benchmark for comedians attempting to connect with their audience on a personal level. He did this by using humor to relate to regular people.

His humorous personas and popular catchphrases include "Garlic Bread" and "Phoenix Nights." These words have gained notoriety and are frequently used in popular culture, demonstrating his influence on British humour. Kay has proven the continuing appeal of live comedy through her successful stand-up comedy tours and specials. He is often cited by other comedians as an example of how to successfully grow a following base through live appearances.

Along with his stand-up performances, Peter Kay has written and performed in popular TV productions like "Phoenix Nights" and "Car Share." His influence has grown beyond the stand-up stage because to his writing and acting accomplishments. Kay has demonstrated how comedians can use their platform for good social impact through his involvement in humanitarian activities like his "Dance For Life" charity dance-a-thon events, motivating others in the business to follow suit.

Peter Kay made a significant contribution to television, had a great career as a stand-up comedian, and had a personable sense of humor. He has long been a source of inspiration for other comedians and a source of amusement for audiences.

Peter Kay has already made a lasting impression on the comedy and entertainment industries. Some elements of his legacy and influence up to that moment are listed below. Kay had a devoted following thanks to his distinct kind of observational comedy, which was distinguished by its relatability and hilarity in ordinary circumstances. He was praised for his comedic skill because of his capacity to find humor in the banal aspects of life.

Peter Kay enjoyed great success with his stand-up comedy tours, and he set records for some of the biggest and most popular comedy performances in the UK. His capacity to fill arenas to capacity and engage a wide range of fans underlined his continuing appeal. Television and Writing: Kay's contributions to the world of television go well beyond stand-up comedy. His successful sitcom

"Phoenix Nights" and critically acclaimed "Car Share" both enjoyed success. His accomplishments as a writer and performer increased his impact outside of the comedy stage.

Peter Kay was renowned for his philanthropic efforts and achievements. His "Dance For Life" charity dance-a-thon events demonstrated his dedication to having a positive impact beyond comedy by raising considerable cash for numerous philanthropic causes. Many comics were inspired by Peter Kay's popularity and style of comedy because they respected his capacity to engage audiences and find funny in everyday situations. Newer generations of comedians have been motivated by his legacy as a performer and comedian.

Printed in Great Britain
by Amazon